Outnumbered

Davy Crockett's Final Battle at the Alamo

Eric Fein

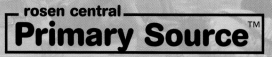

rosen central
Primary Source™

The Rosen Publishing Group, Inc., New York

Published in 2004 by The Rosen Publishing Group, Inc.
29 East 21st Street, New York, NY 10010

Editor: Jennifer Silate
Book Design: Michelle Innes
Photo researcher: Rebecca Anguin-Cohen
Series photo researcher: Jeff Wendt

Photo Credits: Cover (left), title page, p. 22 © Hulton/Archive/Getty Images; cover (right) illustration © Debra Wainwright/The Rosen Publishing Group; p. 6 © Bettmann/Corbis; p. 10 courtesy of Texas State Archives/The UT Institute of Texan Cultures at San Antonio; p. 14 © North Wind Picture Archives; p. 18 Library of Congress, Washington D.C., USA/Bridgeman Art Library; p. 29 The San Jacinto Museum of History, Houston, Texas; p. 30 Tennessee State Museum, Tennessee Historical Society Collection; p. 31 © Center for American History, University of Texas, Austin, TX; p. 32 Texas State Library, Austin, Texas

First Edition

Library of Congress Cataloging-in-Publication Data

Fein, Eric.
    Outnumbered: Davy Crockett's final battle at the Alamo / Eric Fein.—
    1st ed.
    v. cm.—(Great moments in American history)
    Contents: A new adventure — Davy Crockett goes to Texas — Trouble comes to San Antonio — The battle begins!—Remember the Alamo!
    ISBN 0-8239-4347-X (lib. bdg.)
    1. Alamo (San Antonio, Tex.)—Siege, 1836—Juvenile literature. 2. Crockett, Davy, 1786-1836—Juvenile literature. [1. Alamo (San Antonio, Tex.)—Siege, 1836. 2. Texas—History—To 1846. 3. Crockett, Davy, 1786-1836. 4. Pioneers.] I. Title. II. Series.

F390.F37 2004
976.4'03—dc21

2003002686

Manufactured in the United States of America

Contents

Preface 4

1 A New Adventure 7

2 Davy Crockett Goes
  to San Antonio 11

3 Trouble Comes to
  Town 15

4 The Battle Begins! 19

5 Remember the Alamo! 23

Glossary 27

Primary Sources 28

Preface

❦

Davy Crockett was a famous American hunter, soldier, and congressman who lived in the 1800s. Stories about his adventures were told throughout the United States. In November 1835, Davy Crockett left his home state of Tennessee for Texas to begin a new adventure. He was forty-nine years old.

Mexico had ruled Texas since 1821. That year, Mexico won its independence from Spain. Texas and Mexico had been under Spain's rule. Texas became a troubled area for Mexico. Native Americans who lived there often fought with the Mexicans who moved into the area. The Mexican government started allowing Americans to live in Texas. The Mexicans hoped that the Native Americans would fight with them less if American settlers were in Texas, too.

Soon, there were so many American settlers that the Mexican government began to worry that it would lose control of Texas. They made the American settlers follow Mexican laws and become Mexican citizens.

In 1830, Mexico tried to stop settlers from coming to Texas. Mexican soldiers were sent to Texas to try to control the people there. In 1833, Santa Anna became president of Mexico. Many of the people living in Texas did not like Santa Anna. The Texans also wanted independence from Mexico. Fighting started between Mexican soldiers and the Texans. Santa Anna sent more soldiers into Texas. In 1835, the Texans took over the city of San Antonio from the Mexicans. San Antonio was one of the biggest cities in Texas. Winning San Antonio put them closer to that goal. It was at this time that Davy Crockett went to Texas. There he found the greatest adventure of his life....

Davy Crockett was known all over the
United States for his skills as a hunter.

Chapter One

A NEW ADVENTURE

O n November 10, 1835, the pub at the Union Hotel in Memphis, Tennessee, was packed with people. In the center of the crowd stood Davy Crockett. He and his friends were having a party. The party was for him. He was leaving Tennessee the next day for Texas. "Why are you going to Texas, Davy?" a friend asked.

"I am going to Texas because the people of Tennessee have picked someone else to be their congressman," said Crockett. "It is time for me to find a new adventure. There is a lot of land in Texas. I'm going to buy some and make my fortune."

"Aren't you worried about the problems in Texas right now?" another friend asked. "They say Santa Anna is getting ready for a fight."

"Santa Anna does not scare me. I have fought before and I will fight again if I have to," answered Crockett.

Before the sun rose the next morning, Crockett walked to the ferry on Wolf Creek. A group of friends he called the Tennessee Boys were going with him to Texas. They were waiting for him at the dock. Once everyone was on the ferry, the ferryman pushed away from the dock. The ferry floated off toward the Mississippi River. Davy Crockett's trip had begun.

After crossing the Mississippi, Crockett and his friends rode on horseback through Arkansas to the northern part of Texas. They rode through Texas for weeks. Almost every town that Davy visited welcomed him with great dinners and parties. Davy loved being in Texas. There were plenty of bison and bears for him to hunt, and the land was perfect for raising cows. Davy volunteered to become a member of the Texan army when he got to the city of San Augustine. He wrote to his children to tell them about Texas.

My dear son and daughter:

I have safely arrived in Texas. The land is beautiful. I have volunteered to be a soldier for the new government here. When Texas is free from Mexico, I hope to be picked as a member of Texas's government. I should also get a good bit of land for my work in the army. I hope to make my fortune from it. Do not worry about me. I have many friends here.
Love,
Your Father

Crockett and several other men started off for the town of San Antonio. Texan soldiers and U.S. soldiers had recently taken control of the town away from the Mexican army. Mexico's leader, General Santa Anna, had said that he would return to San Antonio. He wanted the city back—and he was willing to fight for it.

Like Davy Crockett, William Travis also came to Texas to find land and his fortune.

Chapter Two

DAVY CROCKETT GOES TO SAN ANTONIO

On February 8, 1836, Davy Crockett and his men spotted small, white buildings through the drizzling rain. "That must be San Antonio," Crockett said to his friends. He wiped the rain from his face with his sleeve. When he looked again, he saw a man on horseback charging in their direction.

"Who are you? And why are you here?" shouted the man, raising his gun into the air.

The leader of the group smiled and said, "My name is Davy Crockett. These men are John Harris, Micajah Autry, Daniel Cloud, and B. Archer Thomas. Are you Colonel Neill, the leader of the soldiers of San Antonio?"

The rider's eyes widened. "Forgive me,

Mr. Crockett. I did not know it was you! I am not Colonel Neill. I am Jim Bowie, a soldier from San Antonio. Welcome," he said.

"Good to be here," replied Crockett.

"Let me help you find a place to rest in town," said Bowie. "Follow me." With that, he turned his horse around and led the men toward San Antonio.

Two days after Crockett arrived in San Antonio, a great party was held for him. Music filled the air. The people of San Antonio danced late into the night. Around 1:00 A.M., a scout burst into the party holding a letter. William Barret Travis, an officer, read the letter. The letter said that Santa Anna was leading about four thousand soldiers toward San Antonio. They would arrive in about two weeks. The letter was written four days before. This meant that the soldiers in San Antonio had less than ten days to get ready for battle. "This doesn't look good," Travis said. "We only have about one hundred and fifty men here who can fight.

But, let's worry about that tomorrow. Tonight, we dance!" The party went on until 7:00 A.M.

On February 11, Colonel Neill found out that someone in his family was very sick. After putting William Travis in charge, he left San Antonio. Some of the soldiers did not like Travis. They did not want to take orders from him. Travis was a regular soldier of the U.S. Army, not a volunteer like most of the others. Travis agreed to let the volunteers pick their own leader. He agreed to share command with whomever was picked.

The volunteers turned to Davy Crockett. They wanted him to be their leader. "Thanks, but I promised Colonel Neill that I would follow his orders," Crockett said. "He put Travis in charge, so I will follow Travis."

Instead, the volunteers picked Bowie to be their leader. Bowie and Travis worked together to get the soldiers ready for battle.

The armies that used the Alamo as a fort made its walls tall and thick to keep out their enemies.

Chapter Three

TROUBLE COMES TO TOWN

Willaim Travis placed Daniel Cloud in the high tower of the church that was in the main plaza of San Antonio. Cloud's job was to ring the bell if he saw the enemy coming. Around noon, on February 23, Cloud saw sunlight reflect off something in the distance. Soldiers were coming! He rang the bell wildly. The clanging of the bell was heard throuhout San Antonio. Travis sent two scouts, John Smith and John Sutherland, to see what was happening. At the same time, Travis ordered everyone in San Antonio to go to the Alamo. He hoped that everyone would be safe there.

At one time, the Alamo had been a Spanish mission. Over the years, the Spanish and the Mexicans had used it as a military fort. The Alamo had white stone walls. Some of the walls of the Alamo

were two feet thick and twelve feet high. There were openings in the walls from which guns and cannons could be fired. About twenty cannons were set up around the Alamo.

When Smith and Sutherland returned, Travis asked, "What did you see?"

"It's bad," replied Sutherland. "There are many Mexican soldiers. They're ready for war."

Travis wrote a letter to the men of Gonzales, the nearest American settlement. He was asking for help. Travis gave the letter to Sutherland. "Do you think you can get this to the town of Gonzales?" Travis asked. "They might be able to send soldiers to help us."

Sutherland took the letter. "I won't let you down, sir," he said.

Later that day, Crockett, Travis, and the other soldiers watched the Mexican army march into San Antonio. One of the Mexican soldiers hung a red flag from the church tower.

"What does the red flag mean?" a young Texan soldier asked Davy Crockett.

"It means that they want to kill us all," answered Crockett. He saw the look of fear on the young man's face. Crockett put a hand on the young man's shoulder. "They're just trying to scare us," he said. "Old Santa Anna is going to wish he stayed home. You'll see."

Crockett and Travis looked at each other. "They think we're just going to lay down our guns," said Travis. "Let's show them how wrong they are. Fire, now!"

BOOM! A cannonball from one of the Alamo's cannons shot high into the air. The Mexican soldiers scattered to get out of its way. Then they fired back. Their bullets rained down on the Alamo. "Come on, men!" screamed Crockett as he loaded another cannon. "Never give up the Alamo!"

And so began one of the most famous battles in U.S. history.

The men inside the Alamo tried to defend their fort against the Mexicans, but they were outnumbered.

Chapter Four

THE BATTLE BEGINS!

S oon after the fighting began, Davy Crockett saw a Mexican soldier near the west wall of the Alamo. The man was about two hundred yards away. Crockett raised his gun. He took aim and fired—the Mexican soldier fell dead.

"He's the first to die!" cheered one of the men standing near Crockett.

"Yes, he is, and he won't be the last!" shouted Crockett, loudly.

The next day, Jim Bowie became so ill that he could not walk. He had to stay in bed for the rest of the battle. Travis was now the only person in charge of all the soldiers. The fighting lasted all day and night for several days. The Mexican army shot cannons at the Alamo. Stones tumbled as the

cannonballs broke through the fort's walls. At night, the men in the Alamo worked to fix the walls with mud and anything else they could find.

On February 27, Crockett got another chance to show off his shooting skills. He spotted Santa Anna with some of the Mexican troops. Crockett fired at the general, making Santa Anna run for cover.

During breaks in the fighting, Crockett tried to keep the Texan soldiers calm. He told funny stories and played his fiddle to make his men feel better.

On March 1, thirty-two men from Gonzales were able to slip past the Mexican soldiers to join the men at the Alamo. Now, there were 189 men to defend the Alamo. Over the next few days, however, the Mexican army blocked all ways into the fort. On March 3, about one thousand Mexican soldiers arrived to strengthen Santa Anna's forces. There were now

about five thousand Mexican soldiers around the Alamo. Travis's hopes that more men would be able to get into the Alamo to help the Texan soldiers were gone.

The Mexican army kept firing cannonballs at the Alamo. The cannonballs began to break through the walls faster than the men in the Alamo could fix them. Over the next two days, March 4 and 5, the Mexican army kept up its attack on the Alamo.

Inside the Alamo, people were worried. They knew there was little chance that they would leave the Alamo alive. Crockett wanted to run out of the Alamo and attack the Mexican army. "If I'm going to die, I want to die out there, fighting like a man. I don't want to be trapped in this fort like an animal," he said to his men.

Unfortunately, Crockett never got his wish.

Once the Mexican soldiers got inside the Alamo, men fought hand to hand. Davy Crockett, shown here with his gun raised, led the fighting.

REMEMBER THE ALAMO!

The evening of March 5 was unusually quiet. Fighting had stopped for the night. The men inside the Alamo continued to fix the damaged walls in any way that they could. Travis looked at the weapons they had left. The men had plenty of guns. However, they did not have enough cannonballs or bullets to stop a large attack by the Mexicans. Travis walked around the fort. He checked with each guard to make sure all was well.

"Good evening, Travis," Crockett said as he looked out into the dark night.

"Seen anything tonight?" asked Travis.

"No, I haven't seen a thing," replied Crockett. "It's too quiet. I think they're up to something."

Travis left Crockett to speak to the other guards. They were as ready as they could be. There was

nothing more to do but wait. Around 3:00 A.M., Travis lay down in his bed. He wore his clothes so that he would be ready if the enemy attacked.

Later that morning, the Mexicans made their move. No one in the Alamo heard or saw them coming. The Mexican soldiers surrounded the Alamo. They were now only about one hundred yards away.

At 5:30 A.M., Travis's door flew open. "The Mexicans are coming!" an officer yelled. Travis jumped from his bed and grabbed his gun. He ran up a dirt ramp to the top of one of the Alamo's walls. He could see Mexican soldiers rushing toward the Alamo from all four sides. They carried ladders that they had made to climb up the Alamo's high walls. Travis's heart pounded in his chest.

"Come on, men! Fire!" he screamed as he raised his gun. Travis shot at the rushing Mexican soldiers. Bullets flew back at Travis. One struck him in the head. Travis dropped to the ground. He was one of the first Texan soldiers in the Alamo to die.

Meanwhile, Davy Crockett was on another wall with his trusty gun, Old Betsy. He shot and reloaded his gun as fast as he could. Bullets screamed past him, but he did not stop firing. Suddenly, the center of the northern wall crumbled. Mexican soldiers poured into the Alamo. Crockett jumped down from the wall to fight the Mexicans entering the fort.

"Get them, men! Never give up the Alamo!" yelled Crockett as he charged a Mexican soldier.

When their guns were out of bullets, Crockett and his men used them as clubs. Crockett fought with all of his might, but there were too many Mexican soldiers. Davy Crockett died while trying to save the Alamo.

The final attack on the Alamo took about one and a half hours. The sun rose at about 7:00 A.M. on March 6, 1836. The early morning light revealed a horrible scene: Dead soldiers lay everywhere in and around the Alamo. Mexican soldiers searched every room for Texan soldiers who were still alive. When they found Bowie in his sickbed, they killed him immediately.

During the battle, the women and children had hidden in the Alamo's church. Luckily, the Mexican soldiers allowed them to leave unharmed.

During the fighting, Santa Anna had been a safe distance away. Now, he entered the Alamo to see what had happened. All of the Alamo defenders had died. About five hundred Mexican soldiers had also been killed or wounded.

News of the fall of the Alamo spread quickly throughout Texas. Instead of scaring the people of Texas, however, this defeat moved them to action.

On April 21, Sam Houston and about four hundred soldiers attacked Santa Anna and a small group of his men at the San Jacinto River. During the battle, the Texas soldiers cried, "Remember the Alamo!" After the battle at San Jacinto, Santa Anna signed a treaty that gave Texas its independence. The brave actions of Davy Crockett had helped the Texans win their war with Mexico.

GLOSSARY

bullet (BUL-it) a small, pointed metal object fired from a gun

cannon (KAN-uhn) a heavy gun that fires large metal balls

cannonball (KAN-uhn-bal) a large, metal ball fired from a cannon

congressman (KONG-griss-man) a person who works for Congress, the body of the United States government that makes laws

defend (di-FEND) to keep something safe from harm

ferry (FER-ee) a boat or ship that regularly carries people across a stretch of water

ferryman (FER-ee-man) someone who runs a ferry

fort (FORT) a building that is strongly built to survive attacks

mission (MISH-uhn) a church or other place where missionaries live and work

volunteer (vol-uhn-TIHR) to offer to do a job, usually without pay; someone who does a job without pay

weapons (WEP-uhnz) things, such as swords, guns, knives, or bombs, that can be used in a fight to attack or defend

yards (YARDZ) units of length equal to 3 feet or .914 meters

Primary Sources

How do we know the details about events that happened long ago in the past? Often we can study clues, such as letters, diaries, and maps, that were written or drawn by the people who were involved in those events. For example, by reading William Barret Travis's letter on page 32, we learn of his concerns about the advancing Mexican soldiers and his promise to never give up the Alamo. Travis's letter helps us to identify the strong feelings he had about the fight against the Mexicans.

Another clue is the map on page 31. The map shows us what the land around the Alamo looked like in 1836. It shows us details such as where the Alamo and other buildings in San Antonio were located. Historical maps, such as this one, help us describe how an area looked many years ago. These and other kinds of clues bring the past to life so that we can learn what happened more than 150 years ago at the Alamo.

After Santa Anna (above) was captured in San Jacinto, U.S. president Andrew Jackson returned him to Mexico. However, he was no longer allowed to be president of Mexico.

Powder horns were used to carry gunpowder, a powder used to fire guns. Davy Crockett used this powder horn for his gun.

Santa Anna used this map to help him plan his attack. The Alamo is in the upper left. The town of San Antonio is shown below the Alamo on the other side of the San Antonio River.

During the second day of the battle, Travis sent this letter to "The People of Texas and All Americans in the World." In the letter, Travis promised to never give up the fight for independence.